Praise for *Gun/Shy*

"Jim Daniels is one of our best chroniclers of an American past that is, for better and worse, gone. As such, his is a poetry that laments and celebrates our present moment—its people, the lives they live, the ideas they live by, and the places, people, and things they call theirs. When one of his speakers says, 'Today, / I'm just watching. Carried away,' you realize a pact has been made (between the speaker and world) and a promise fulfilled (by the poet for the reader): that these poems will carry you away, that the voice behind them 'wants to kneel on the floor / and whisper a prayer / like in the old days.' Now more than ever, we need those prayers, and these poems."

—Hayan Charara, author of *Something Sinister*

"In this new collection by one of our country's best poets, Daniels brings us the news from this world and transforms it into the news from beyond this world. These are poems of time and place, written in familiar voices, suggesting narratives that could be our own, but he's infused each line, each poem, with mystery and music. These are poems that escape their form, and remake themselves in the reader's mind—in our moment and in our memory. This is poetry that inspires and terrifies. These lines are poignant, unforgettable, resonant, but somehow remain conversational, as if this poet is simply tossing off brilliance with each new observation, each sharp image. This is the strongest collection yet from one of our most important poets."

—Laura Kasischke, author of *The Time Machine*

"Daniels' *Gun/Shy* is a journey. It is not just a book of poems, but a long journey from his childhood home of Warren and Detroit to adulthood, where somewhere along this long journey, the city evolved even as the author or we all evolved. There is something profound about Jim Daniels' ability to humble us through poetry that is self-effacing at a moment in history where we most need to step away from ourselves in order to know the larger world outside of us. These powerful poems will make you laugh, wonder, pause, but long after you have laid the book down, deep inside your heart, they will reveal something profound about the way we all become survivors. This is an urgently necessary book coming to us at such a time."

—Patricia Jabbeh Wesley, author of *Praise Song for My Children: New and Selected Poems*

"Jim Daniels' poetry explores not only the realities of a blue-collar, late twentieth-century, upper Midwest childhood, but the entirety of America's sociocultural whirlwind throughout these last six decades. Few writers believe more deeply in poetry's capacity to document the world, and documentation, in his hands, is a form of homage. Sure, *Gun/Shy* is a new chapter in Daniels' grand, literary-historical project—more importantly, it is an essential collection from one of our contemporary masters."

—Campbell McGrath, Philip and Patricia Frost Professor of Creative Writing, Distinguished University Professor of English, Florida International University

GUN/SHY

Made in Michigan Writers Series

GENERAL EDITORS

Michael Delp, Interlochen Center for the Arts
M. L. Liebler, Wayne State University

A complete listing of the books in this series can be
found online at wsupress.wayne.edu

GUN/SHY

JIM DANIELS

WAYNE STATE UNIVERSITY PRESS
DETROIT

ISBN 978-0-8143-4878-9 (paperback)
ISBN 978-0-8143-4879-6 (ebook)

Library of Congress Control Number: 2021934647

Publication of this book was made possible by a generous gift from The Meijer Foundation.

Cover design by Tracy Cox

Wayne State University Press rests on Waawiyaataanong, also referred to as Detroit, the ancestral and contemporary homeland of the Three Fires Confederacy. These sovereign lands were granted by the Ojibwe, Odawa, Potawatomi, and Wyandot Nations, in 1807, through the Treaty of Detroit. Wayne State University Press affirms Indigenous sovereignty and honors all tribes with a connection to Detroit. With our Native neighbors, the press works to advance educational equity and promote a better future for the earth and all people.

Wayne State University Press
Leonard N. Simons Building
4809 Woodward Avenue
Detroit, Michigan 48201-1309

Visit us online at wsupress.wayne.edu

CONTENTS

1. Hamburger Surprise

2. Street View

3. Gun/Shy

4. Leaving the Piano Behind

5. The Grand Design

UNWRITTEN LAWS OF GRAVITATIONAL ISOLATION

Warren, Michigan

Imagine rows of magnetic houses spaced each
to each against the curb like stones on a path leading
to lemmings' cliff. Each magnet not attracted
or repelled, but anchored to the earth.

So close to each other, we could hold hands
through open windows, linked by force fields
of sweat. But why hold hands, that embarrassing
empty exercise that strained the heart's unused

muscles and caused someone to give up under
duress or mockery? Do magnets breathe? We were
that close and that far away in a pattern determined
by Monopoly men and Factory men and Families

in the Game of Life with babies squeezed into cars
with imaginary seatbelts and piles of counterfeit
money and family photographs. The point is, we had
no need to sharpen our knives to cut through butter

and the soft lies of upward mobility. We were always
sinking, even during fire drills for the census. The point
is, dullness was a virtue and virtue was a poorly worded
document subject to invalid erasures and brick walls

mortared with the froth of betrayal. We never
borrowed cups of sugar, or bedpans—or expired curses,
though they still worked if we spit them out quick
enough. When the scoreboard ran into overtime

we forgot our casual hatreds. Our parents never
crossed each other's thresholds. Buy-one-get-one-free
was the golden rule, but it turned out to be copper
and Abraham Lincoln turned out to be Liberace.

Maybe I shouldn't say *never*. Maybe I should
asterisk it in case I missed some violation
of the threshold. I hate to admit, maybe
we were too tired to get it up for an affair.

Maybe the men, too tired from work, maybe
the women, too tired of us, the Catholic mass
of children of the damned, the Catholic math
of carry the one, adding another child—

were we what kept the fire burning, or remnants
of that fire? That'll keep you up at night, rubbing
your hands together over the magnets, hoping
for a cure for magic. An electric burn shocked us

inside out when someone died on the block
or bled enough to bring the cops—that
brought us outside, following on our bikes
at a distance, circling the circled bloodstains

in the aftermath. Maybe the point is, we knew
what was where in each other's houses,
from toilet to TV, to unused wedding presents
we passed on to each other in lieu of pleasantries.

Maybe the point is, it was our blood.

1

HAMBURGER SURPRISE

SUNDAY BEST

Something men did. Taught their sons. Made a mess.
Newspaper spread on the kitchen floor. Pale green
tile swirled with white and black, camouflage
for spills and stains. The tins of Shinola, the brushes,
the polishing rage. Rags. Rage. Walls cigarette-
yellow. The religion of blending in, passed down
by generations who performed with robotic clarity
to an audience of auto parts, who punched time clocks
and drove home and scrubbed up and slept
or stayed out and drank and either way punched
in again the next day. Applying the polish, rubbing it in,
buffing one shoe, the other. For Sunday. God's strange
ideas about purity involved the distinction between
shit and Shinola. Shoes for the Church of No Fun.
God wore a fedora and docked your pay, since time
told no lies. Our father, who art polishing his shoes,
one hand in a shoe, the other on a brush. The slashing
slap against it, he taught us—satisfying in a way
that did not involve fists. Four boys waiting our turns
at the polish tin. A shine we could see in lieu of shame.
Shame-ola. Looking down, like we always did.
His were steel-toed, cheap from the plant store.
You couldn't tell unless you stepped on them.
You'd think they'd last forever, and you'd be right.
My grandfather unscrewed spikes off golf shoes
he found at Goodwill to wear on special occasions.
You'd forget until he put his feet up. I wore down
football spikes dragging them over cement
riding my bike home from practice to send up sparks.
Can you see me back then, uncamouflaged in dim light
in front of the high school? Spark-ola. Polish-smeared
newsprint—want ads, obits, the funnies. I've lost
my way, my black tracks. One year we got plastic shoes
from Goodwill, or St. Vincent de Paul, or Salvation Army,
my memory smeared by camouflage. You can't
polish plastic shoes, we learned as it smeared
like sin on the surface. Nothing could penetrate—
just scratch and scuff. Polish marred the tile floors

of church that day we wore them, shuffling past
the holy water and slumping into a long empty row
near the back, as always. On our way out, we saw
the streaks we'd made. We pretended it was always
that way, which is as good a camouflage as anything.

My Mother at the Sewing Machine

hums through drifting motes
of dim-light dust through
basement window wells,
and the odd magic of us alone
together—daytime, weekday.
Sick, I shiver with fevered clarity.
She is sewing arrows on a scout uniform.
She is rustling pinned patterned fabric
through the machine for my sister's dress.
She is she is she is: bobbin spin, needle thread
and the near-invisible orange suck
on her cigarette while her hands run fabric.
She is sewing inches of jeans from one
ruined pair onto the blown-out knees
of another. Four boys—the jeans must last.
My mother at the sewing machine
in cold basement light where I lie
on the itchy sponge of an old sofa
watching my deaf grandmother's
tiny TV with the sound off
while upstairs she shuffles into idle.
My mother stuck between us
threads another needle.
In that quiet glow,
I could be sick for weeks.

STUFFING THE BIRDS, CARNEGIE
NATURAL HISTORY MUSEUM

I zigzagged the double stroller up the handicap ramp
and into the elevator to the third floor where birds posed

in permanent peace, forever on the verge of flight. I let
the children loose, the waxed tile floor echoing winter boots

as they stumbled forward, hooting bird calls from distant planets,
arms willfully flapping. Dusty dioramas, relegated to a remote

corridor, while a floor below us, children lined up to scream
at computerized dinosaurs. Time kicked back while my children

smudged glass, ignoring names, habitats, migration patterns.
My son learned to whistle, my daughter learned to snap her fingers,

but the birds stood still. Leaning between vulture and eagle,
I envied my children's ability to fill silence with birdsong,

my own wings shrugged off long ago. They roamed the rows
while I stood in imitation of forced permanence, extinction's

camouflage. When they tired, I strapped them back in
and pushed home through December slush or January's

crisp refusal to acknowledge us. Their flights cannot be
measured accurately without carbon dating and love.

Our state bird, the ruffed grouse, though we'll never
see one in our pigeoned city. Nests, abandonment,

prey, predator. Back home, I gave them juice boxes
and cookies. I read them another fairy tale about forever.

About children who flew, who paid no price.

POTATO SKINS

Steam rose from broken skins
like sentimental music.
None of us played or sang
or even hummed in our house.
If my father was home, we said grace.
If he wasn't, silence sufficed.

Our deaf grandmother could've
broke our hearts if she hadn't
cut so many farts. She hunched
into prayer, surrounded
by mad lambs of God.

■■■

I breathed in steam, the off-
white flesh, the brief tangled
substance of heat. A hard stick
of margarine passed in ritual
agitation as things quickly cooled.

Love's harsh mirage dissipated
as we bumped elbows and squirmed
around the tiny table, three of us
squeezed on the long bench
against the wall like panelists
on a canceled game show.

■■■

We loved the skins, rough
jackets pocketed with melted
margarine so when we bit, yellow
spilled down our chins—five children,
my mother, my grandmother, and my
he'll-eat-when-he-gets-home.

Meatloaf and baked potatoes.
God and all of his incarnations.

Body and blood. Carnal communion.
So what if we called it butter
and forgot to wipe our chins?

We put our faces in the steam
and we wept.

RETURNING THE STONES

Pictured Rocks National Lakeshore

The children, five and four, built cushioned
forts from matching love seats in company
housing in Marquette where we lived on one
of many temporary assignments. No wars
or even minor skirmishes on that soft battlefield.

Each time we hit the beach, they collected a thick
heft of colored stones and carried back pockets
and handfuls to gently stack outside our apartment
like the impossible eggs of some extinct waterbird.

We took a boat tour of the Pictured Rocks and, stunned
by the land's rugged rainbows jutting into the storm
of dark waters, I confessed to dumping their pretty rocks
back into the cold, cold lake. My son cried and hit me.

I didn't understand children need ballast to hold
and wish on, and how water, which can take away
life, brings all things to it. Oh, the daily casualties
stagger us now, the same list of our four names, over
and over. I should have let them keep the rocks.

How odd it must have looked, a grown man throwing
rock after rock from two large canvas sacks
back into the water like God's quality control inspector.
They do not even remember the weighted comfort
of that summer—what would not break, not split in two.

My Father Worked 800 Hours of Overtime

on the line at Ford's the year I turned 16
and had sex with a substitute teacher
and began drinking in earnest
and selling nickel bags
out of the basement bean bag chair.

800=20 extra 40-hour weeks.
Using the math invented by the state
of Michigan to lower the drinking age
to 18, that gave me 15 more hours
per week at the gates of oblivion.

Oblivion was a mirage state
between Michigan and Ohio.
You had to close your eyes
and pick an exit off of I-75.
Oblivion had no gates.

My father quit smoking
after three friends from work
died in a six-month span.
The cartons of Marlboros
disappeared from the closet

leaving me to my own devices
of retail theft and cadging. I couldn't
smoke my mother's Kools—
menthol was for girls. She could
either quit smoking or leave

my father. Story problems
like crickets in the basement,
mice in the kitchen, rats in the trash,
untranslatable and breeding
with the frenzy of ex-smokers.

Working at the same plant, I never
approached his record or even called to it
from a distance. I drove south on I-75
and almost approached Canada
before swerving toward Ohio, speeding

right through the mirage of my own
future 800 hours away. Getting high
in Marlboro Country, spooking the horses,
stampeding them into stalled rust buckets
abandoned on the I-75 service drive.

I ended up in the middle of a funeral
procession heading out to the distant cemetery
where an actuary handed me a ticket
and offered condolences. Father,
I imagine you tallying up those hours,

in lieu of love, in lieu of vacation, in lieu
of even mowing the damn lawn, throwing
an extra buck in the church envelopes resting
in their box next to the coffin of Kools.
God and overtime. Abandoning

the Usher's Club and Holy Name Society
to give your reluctant work-ship to the hymns
of Henry Ford who hated Jews loved money
and went camping with Thomas Edison
where they rubbed two workers together

to start their fire. My father as match head.
800 hours. His hobby? Staying alive.
Stranded in the rush hour of his own life.
Laws were broken. Canada was avoided.
Detroit, the only place in the continental U.S.

north of Canada. Some nights I waited up for him
in the dark house, then ran to bed to escape
his headlights' glare. Some nights I was out
and had to sneak back in, waiting for him
to finish his solitary beer in the yellow kitchen

while finishing my own, parked out front
in my Plymouth Satellite in the darkness
of the busted streetlight. I missed the smell
of Marlboros when he quit, the comfort
of ash, the burn that meant he'd been there.

WASTING MY LIFE, 3:00 A.M.

The cool burn of cigarette
smoke swirled in my lungs
late night passing by the street-
light in front of my own dwelling

in favor of the orange period
in my fingers, the end
to every silent sentence.
An uncertain squeeze held it

between two fingers used,
most often, to turn it up.
It: all things not gentle.
In favor of one more time

around the block to buy
myself more time alone
to memorize what I might
say if you asked again

what I might do
with my life, as you smelled
the smoke on me,
the burning.

THE NEW MATH

On the basement futon, my daughter
squeezes my hand through yet
another kids' movie killing off the dad

which prompts a long conversation
in which tallies are taken, dead mothers
vs. dead fathers. Nothing happens

if the parents stick around. I've been writing
the new year on checks, and I don't like it.
Damn is acceptable in children's films,

but not *shit. Hell?* Yes. Yet try explaining limbo
to a seven-year-old. Like a bowling ball rolling
down one endless alley, kiddie bumpers up,

no gutter to fall into. Their real dads sit back
raking in the dough their kids make *acting*!
I'm developing a fondness for the exclamation

point. Look kids, I'm not tired! I'm not sleeping!
Just because God isn't talking to you and me
doesn't mean he's not out there keeping score.

Shucks, I'm back in a Western again. Somebody
has to be the sheriff's kids, and I'm deputizing
you and you. When I was a kid, we had no

futons or streaming. But we had guardian angels
and undisputed national champions.
Okay, your dad's a fibber. But, say the moon

is your bowling ball, wouldn't you want to
just grab it and hold on? I'm going to die,

regardless of punctuation. Like in the movies.
And you'll have some great adventure

called the rest of your life. Me, I'll be popcorn
stars and bad reception. When you're lying in bed
late at night, whisper to me the latest equations.

BAHIA HONDA, KEY WEST

We're snorkeling on a reef—choppy
    water almost canceled the trip.
My son, eighteen, beautiful fish—

chest sprouting sleek hair
    gangly god treading his future
without us. He points at flamboyant fish

in their silent raucous confetti spray
    and I nod vigorously
and point back to make sure of some

thing passing between us
    till my snorkel clogs
due to vigorous nodding. We do not

stray far from the boat or each other
    though the dizzy current pulls
us apart. We cannot name the many fish

but we can name each other in that deep
    underwater silence of murmuring hearts.
We tire, as we must, and flop back

onto the boat for the long ride
    to the dock. Lord, I have never
been so tired, so awake, his cold shoulder

touching mine on the crowded boat,
    his slight lean toward me
then away. Last night we passed

the B&B in Key West—where
    he was conceived,
my wife told him. *TMI*, he blurted out.

She could not help herself
      in sight of that single moment
of silent glistening. Today for two hours

the world's just water, breath, air.
      We move our arms. We swim for it.

I LOVE WATCHING RIVERS

I'm not fussy. Any body
of rushing water. 300 miles away,
my parents meet with a briefcased
man to settle their affairs on their way

out the door, so we don't kill each other
trying to do it ourselves—us, the kids,
and it, dividing the meager spoils
with the clawed hands of grudge.

We ourselves prepare to retire,
take the package, shred the paper,
wave goodbye or give the finger, or both.
The river never waves goodbye.

The Monongahela after spring rain—
high ripples, brown churn.
I hear that long-gone fish are returning
to cleaner waters. Long-gone faith

returning. Going against the current
has never been our style. My parents,
nervous to meet the man, relieved
when he's gone. Blowing in the wind,

they grip the clothesline. Lists shorten
in my father's neat script. My blind
mother scrawls in overlapping hieroglyphics
we try to decipher when the mailman guesses

right and drops her letters into our boxed hearts.
We name our rivers, but I think of them
as one constant unnamed thing in the face
of all we name, in the face of calculated distance.

The man with the briefcase is headed
my way. Everybody has a lot to say
about rivers, and dying. Today,
I'm just watching. Carried away.

FOG ON THE TURNPIKE

For years, remarkably, no one you know
dies. Those years end. Maybe with your wispy
grandmother breaking her hip or losing her mind,
or both, or maybe with the girl who marked
your neck with your first hickey in seventh grade
then got trapped in a house fire in eighth.

They end in a tiny viewing room in tight shoes,
stomach roiling with boredom/grief/claustrophobic
panic, as if you are the one coffined. Sucker punched,
your gut knows it has begun—the first hard bead
dropping from misery's broken rosary.

It's either your smart-ass uncles reeking of lies
and booze, telling Farting Grandma stories
or the girl's parents doped up—the mother's
contorted wails, a record on permanent warp,
the father's quaking stupor and slur—
but they're over, over, over, and your souvenirs

seem silly, and you count to ten, then stop
counting forever. You outgrow the shoes,
but the next pair waits in the dark closet.
You start taking vitamins seriously, rattling
their maracas. You perform CPR
on your faith in an afterlife.

You regret calling her Farting Grandma,
regret dumping the girl for another
who'd go down on you, shame bruising
your grief even as it numbs. But soon
enough, fog on the turnpike, and the bodies,
crash after crash, pile up.

Moments of impact, brutal slamming
as you head down into it, low visibility,
syntax skewed by choked-back affirmations
of your own survival.

HAMBURGER SURPRISE

It was no surprise to see my mother opening
another can of cream of mushroom soup
while hamburger faded gray, and grease
popped in the cast-iron pan seasoned
by generations of salty language.

■■■

My father felt a bit sheepish
about eating rice. What would
Mr. Potato Head think? Rice,
and any vegetable that didn't emerge
from a can. Even frozen veggies—
he'd claw at the frosty boxes
and sniff them in his paws, suspicious
as a polar bear with a granola bar.

■■■

Raw burger, a little blood-pond
at the bottom of the Styrofoam.
My mother had some surprises
but this wasn't one of them.
We relied on predictable milk money
beneath six lunch bags on the counter
each morning, one firm nickel
we could trust with our lives.

■■■

She was 36, and could they afford
another child? Did the rhythm
of the calendar drop its guard?
She lost that last child
and never had another.

■■■

The first one, my oldest brother—
well, she had a theory

about the Disposable Child,
that it would've helped to have
one to practice on first.

■■■

We could make a long list
of things we never discussed
but who has time for that
with everybody in intensive care
or dying or dead or maybe deadbeat
or floating in the grease
of that frying pan emptied
into the soup can to harden
and be thrown out?

■■■

Five kids, not counting
the stillborn one named Paul.
The name, a little secret.
My mother kept stirring.

2

STREET VIEW

SHOUTING A SONNET INTO
DETROIT'S DEAD MICROPHONE

I don't buy that shit about *giving voice*
to the voiceless promised by The Messiahs
of pitch-perfect windproof hair and invisible
wallets and sugar-free gum.

And hearing aids, well, they're too
damn expensive and easy to lose.
And megaphones and microphones—
tap, tap, tap, is this thing on, can you

hear me out there? And all you get back
is either, *you talking to me?* Or
can you tone it down? Variations
in tone. A luxury sedan speeding away.

Don't blame it on acoustics
or the pensioners or the square mileage
or the ancient infrastructure. I lack
all authority, but I'm just getting started.

Somebody tried to cut me off after fourteen
lines, but I drive fast. And if I shouted
him down, can you blame me? Let's gargle
on vague promises and spit with the authority

of jackhammers. If we're voiceless,
who took those voices? I want to give ears
to the earless. Being tone deaf
is an acquired trait. *It's complicated,*

The Messiahs say. *Plug it in,* I say.
Gotta start somewhere.

SEARCHLIGHTS

On nights when searchlights crossed the sky
I believed in magic and riches, God and fame,
or at least somewhere to go when I died

though the beams only meant a sale at some car lot
on Eight Mile, or Family Night at the ball game—
those nights when searchlights crossed the sky

with bold swords that made brave stars shy.
Some nights on our cracked street I followed their aim
until my mother called me in to tell me lies

like *we're not poor* and *boys don't cry.*
Our lights were dim with no cash and lots of blame.
My father worked nights while searchlights crossed the sky.

When my grandmother fell out of bed, he and I
drove to lift her from the floor and her own shame
for being a burden, hating my mother, wanting to die.

We passed Mel Farr Ford—clear haloes of lights aimed
high looked like nothing we could ever hope to claim
on our way home, below searchlights across the sky,
leaving us nowhere to go when we died.

LEGENDARY TOADS

Most tadpoles are herbivorous. Some species are omnivorous, eating detritus and, whenever available, other tadpoles. Almost all toads of the family Bufonidae have two lumps on either side of the back of their head, called the parotoid glands. These glands release an alkaloid poison, which oozes out if the toad is stressed or frightened.

The only frogs I've ever met
lived as registered guests in Amphibianville
at the zoo. My brothers and I found toads
in the yard and mauled them with our hands.
They spit toad juice on us, toad pee,
whatever—we thought it would kill us,
so it was briefly thrilling. Frogs lived
in ritzier digs, we assumed, though it depends
on how you feel about swamps. We assumed
anything we lacked came down to money.
Except for the poison, the toads seemed
almost stoic about our fondling, tossing,
happy that we never actually stuck
lit firecrackers in their mouths.

■■■

A stream once ran between backyards
when our sub was farmland
according to the ancient farmer
whose tiny house stunk with dying.
Regardless, water pooled there each spring,
bred tadpoles we thought were frogs
till they punched out limbs to become
toads like us. Frogs get all the glory.
People spear them at night. What we
could have done with spears!
We played a game called Kill
the Guy with the Ball
and multiple variations thereof.

■■■

We blended in like toads in dirt and high weeds, believing
it was our nature. On field trips to Amphibianville,
we envied their cool dark shelter, the tiny signs
identifying them by names that we'd never
have ourselves. Even now, my hands itch
for those toads. You won't find them in textbooks,
and only those of us with dirt in our eyes
can even spot them in plain sight.

THE YEAR OF BURNING

The year you—or was it me?—first squinted
into the sun and imagined blindness. The year
we stopped calling our mother's mother "Little Grandma"
when Big Grandma died and made it unnecessary.
The year of highballs with Aunt Betty,
the year Uncle Norm emerged from self-imposed solitary
confinement in his room to take a pee
while we bounced off the thin echo of their shrinking
apartment in Providence Projects while our parents tried
to patch it up at the bar around the corner
and our father brawled with the bouncer. The year
our brother bought a red pickup but picked up nothing,
so got thrown out of the house. Trailer cap on back.
He circled the block late at night. He parked and slept
somewhere beneath that cap. Our father tried
to repair the hole he'd punched in the wall
only to end up with a plaster shrine to anger.
We refined the lost art of the spit in the dusty vacant lot
behind the bowling alley in Warren, on the buffered border
where someone once imagined they'd build something,
but the money oozing out of Detroit wasn't staying
in our neighborhood. Rust-proofing was a joke.
We bit, we spit, we beat each other up
while Grandpa stuck it out alone back in Detroit.
You have to go along, our father said, or get going,
but you're not moving in here. Neither big
nor little, he was our only grandfather. He retired
from unemployment and performed odd jobs
for the priest across the street who blessed his wounds
and took his wallet. We paused for a breath, and the city—
you can go up in flames or down in flames
but Detroit just went in flames—smoke proved
toxic to white skin, and new settlements emerged
in the ancient farmlands of Rochester
and Rochester Hills, where rumor had it
there was once indeed a hill. Our grandfather
dully phoned in reports like a drugged correspondent,
fingering the bullet hole in his window for years

to come—like a lucky ring or the Belgian Boy plugging
the dike in the alternate history of our inadequately
documented ancestry. So I'm here to say
it was all pretty shruggy with oblivion
down in our basement where our black-and-white TV
sold us magic blinders. In other words,
we were giant ants digging into the soft wood
of our own problems. Like, where did Aunt Betty
get that gun, and couldn't she just have poisoned
the old bastard instead and gotten away with it?
And who was that drug dealer in the red pickup
with the cap on top who sold bad acid
to the entire neighborhood until its victims
wandered the streets like birthday clowns
with the wrong address? One afternoon we saw
National Guard helicopters and smelled smoke,
but just went back downstairs to rewatch our favorite reruns.
Big Mom and Big Dad did work things out eventually,
but for a time we lived above the bowling alley
where we jimmied the cigarette machine until we got
caught. And if I've told more lies than you can shake
a stick at, just don't shake that stick. While some serious,
serious shit was going on down the block where the street
crossed into Detroit, I was mastering the "15" puzzle,
and the neighbor girl was learning how to do that thing
with the cherry stem. Big Dad never lost his job, despite
various extended layoffs and aborted fantasies,
and he left us alone if we laid a six-pack on him now
and then. I'm going on the record—even with its drunken
scratches. Grandpa bought up vacant lots around him
for ten bucks apiece from the city. He never planted crops
like he'd imagined. He was a guy who should have drank more
and dreamed less. He invented a fake dog and his own
fire department consisting of one garden hose, carried no wallet
after repeatedly being relieved of it, but still had twenty bucks
pinned inside his shirt pocket, ripped out unceremoniously
by a young man whose bike he'd repaired years earlier
as a hedge against payback, but that young man had nothing

to lose—at least I learned that much. Our grandfather
was our last link to the city, and he died in his sleep,
so maybe one of his dreams did come true. 1967.
All the helicopters full of what, at age eleven,
I should have been learning. If I could go back
I would've read the newspaper
before it burned.

BETWEEN DOUBLE DOORS

We stood inside the main entrance
to Fitzgerald High. *Janis Joplin died,*
somebody said. *Her too?* I said.
Hendrix just two weeks gone.

Too young to have loved either of them.
Homeroom, then first period.
October, and school already sucked.
Why were we stuck sandwiched

between doors? I squeezed my bag lunch.
No cafeteria for me and my brothers.
We'd gone in together on a stereo,
allowed in the basement if we kept it

down. Keeping things down—not
something we did well. Jimi and Janis
weren't big at our school. I wasn't big
myself, thin as a locker, with the heart

of an elf. Maybe elves have big hearts.
Maybe I have to take that back.
Somewhere between the hoods
and the hippies, I fell through cracks

into the DMZ. When was I going to be all
of something? I counted on the cracks. Stuck
between doors while they brought
dogs in to sniff our lockers. I didn't

know much, but I knew not to keep
my stash at school. Jimi and Janis—
the names together almost sang,
like Jack and Jill up that hill.

Tumbling down. Jill tumbling after.
We had no hills in Detroit, nor bikes
without motors. I liked the scream
of them—guitar, voice—searing burn

of my first raging grief when Marlene
died that summer, nowhere near 27.
Listening to them, I smelled the awful
crackle and pop. Basement fire—

dryer pilot, gas spill. Turn it up. Turn it
down. Folded notes from a girl flaking
into ash behind the garage. I wasn't
too young to love drugs.

Even my brothers disapproved.
One a jock, the other a hood.
Janis died. I did not shrug.
You can never get back that pure

loneliness—I keep looking for
a better word, getting lost.
The dark center of a car's lighter
surrounded by the searing orange coil.

Standing in the middle of nowhere
between locked doors, who should
I have listened to? What better than to scream?
I should have. It wouldn't have killed me.

ON A PERSONAL LEVEL

In 1926, shaken by a gang of white men in the Ku Klux Klan, Louis's family moved to Detroit, forming part of the post-World War I great migration. Joe's brother worked for Ford Motor Company where Joe would himself work for a time at the Rouge Plant, and the family settled into a home in Detroit's Black Bottom neighborhood. . . . A memorial to Louis was dedicated in Detroit on October 16, 1986 . . . a 24-foot-long arm with a fisted hand suspended by a 24-foot-high pyramidal framework. It represents the power of his punch both inside and outside the ring.

I tossed massive truck axles from rotating hooks
onto pallets at the end of the assembly line
in the Ford Sterling Plant, eight miles
down Mound Road from the Motor City border
at Eight Mile Road.
     Huh (lift)/ *Uh* (toss)
alternating with another guy to allow
a few seconds of human recovery.
At the end of my first shift, my arms
tingled and ached with numb strings
of sweat as I wobbled toward
the time clock.
     What I want to say is
I lived in a little house, grungy green
siding with aluminum awnings that'd
never be white again due to the nature
of the air from factories like mine.
Why bother scrubbing?
      What I want to say is
I have been *broke with nowhere to go*
and tossing those axles built muscles
from nothing except expired prayers
and the smoky acrid breath of mornings after
exceptionally good whiskey I could not afford.
What I want to say is
     the guy I worked with
was a tall Black kid named Chris from the other
side of Eight Mile who never played sports

as well as his two ambitious uncles imagined, or just
didn't study in school like he needed to—

                                     he alternated versions
of that story like pushing buttons on a jukebox, generous
with his pocketful of unchanging change. Both versions
were true, he said.

                 What I want to say is
when I first started, he sometimes took two axles
in a row to give me more time to recover.

                                 I am always
in recovery, they tell me. Back then, a pallet looked
as good to me as a bed, and a place to stack axles six rows
high, alternating directions, to be carried off by a hi-lo driver
who would die from smoking and his enormous
belly and the bottom-shelf fortified wine he turned
into water every break on afternoons, the alki shift, 3–11.
Perfect, I'd imagined, but Chris warned me often, once
he knew—*straight home, brother*—kept me in line
on the line. He too did not drink. Once I caught up,
he taught me to slow down.

                 What I want to say is
we were not friends. Eight Mile Road hit
with the rough authority of our barbed-wire lives
and a Joe Louis punch. Joe, a Las Vegas greeter
then, died in 1981 in Paradise, Nevada,
not Paradise, Michigan.

MIDNIGHT FOOTBALL

Under one streetlight on concrete
gone quiet on night's a.m. dial
the ball echoes when dropped,
then wobbles to a curb, oh,

we sweat clean, clomping in drunken
boots, steel-toed glorious thumping
as we trudge past parked cars—
buttonhook, crisscross, flare,

down-and-in, down-and-out,
four of us—passer/receiver
rusher/defender, oh, Mississippis
one through five, two-hand shove

we don't *touch* each other, puffing,
hands on knees, in factory shape—
no running—but—hut, hut, hike—
in the air tonight the burn-off of summer

into fall. One of us had been a star
in high school, and watching him run
by me tonight I feel the sad tinny weight
of the announcer calling his name—

I'm not mocking him when I cup my hands:
Touchdown by Logan! We gather
in the pockmarked end zone in the almost-
dark at the edge of the light's soft circle

of breath and do a touchdown dance
not allowed back in school—nobody
keeping score or keeping time through
this brief broken window of our lives.

The neighbors aren't shouting *shut up*—
cool enough tonight for closed windows
maybe, or maybe it's just a home game,
and I know it might be easy or expected

to tell Logan to *go long* when we switch
up teams, but I love to see the man run,
and when I say it's as simple as that, I'm only
lying a little bit. *Go long!* echo rising

like steam to disappear in the dark.
I know better than to say
and keep on going, brother—
our plays more complicated than that.

HARLEM GLOBETROTTERS, OLYMPIA STADIUM

Watch your car for a dollar? Ted's father
glanced around, wearily paid two Black kids.
We parked on one of many snowy streets
without meters or guarantees. The kids
scowled at me and Ted, eye-level.
The scowl earned on the turf
of their Black neighborhood visited
by suburban whites for hockey
or Jethro Tull or Traffic
or basketballers mugging for laughs.

Ted, recently reclassified as the only kid
on the street with divorced parents, reaped
the benefits when his absent father returned
at Christmas with Globetrotter tickets for him
and a friend. The warm-up act: ping-pong
played with methodical exuberance
as the sparse crowd settled, draping coats
over vacant seats. Mr. C's seats, front-row
folding chairs. A ping-pong ball rolled off
the floor, and I palmed it into a pocket.

His father's tickets stamped *Complimentary*
across the stubs he mangled in his fist.
I never learned what he did for a living,
but that too involved cash exchanges—
and long disappearances and tinted glass.

Ping-pong diplomacy—America
versus China, a diorama of a historical event
lost on us. The American won, waving his tiny flag
to squeeze the sparse crowd into polite applause,
then on to "Sweet Georgia Brown." The depantsing
of a Washington General might've caused a riot
if it happened on our street. The bucket of confetti
tossed like water failed to surprise us, though we laughed—
expected. Like the dollar for the car.

Ted and I practiced spinning balls on our fingers.
He mastered that trick, but never the layup, the jump shot,
or even the dribble. He spun himself into dropping out,
then mopped the floors at the Salvation Army
where he stored his life in a locker and watched
our cars for nothing, but asked for dollars on principle,
layered in stink, fueled by tightly wrapped bottles.

You know who won. The white Generals had a job
to do—inept and befuddled. The Globetrotters
hooted. We were all in on the same joke
with different punch lines. The Generals, privates
in the army competing for the entertainment dollar.

In 1967, tanks on the street, helicopters keeping
the beat. The white mayor conferred with the white
governor and police chief. On the edge of the city,
Ted and I counted choppers in the lazy daze of safety—
despite rumors *they* were coming to get *us*.

The Globetrotters were funnier when edited
for *Wide World of Sports*. Isolated laughter
echoed over empty seats under the roof
where Gordie Howe played, though Mr. Hockey
meant nothing to those kids outside.
The hubcaps were gone. So were the kids.
Mr. C shrugged and quietly swore, unarmed
in deference to the occasion. In '67,
he wore a holster, drank beer on his porch,
nodding to neighbors as if they shared
the same secret.

We'd gotten soaked by the confetti
of a contract shredded by our daily myths.
We shook it off and headed toward
the exits. Scoreboards were useless,
as were clocks. Somewhere

someone spun a hubcap on a finger
and evaluated its worth.

On our factory street, no one trotted
the globe, though a lucky few ventured
Up North one week each summer.
What I didn't know could fill the thick,
abandoned program Ted picked up on our way out.

Two kids emerged from shadow to conjure
fear. Fear unacknowledged in translation. Blurred
borders, and a gun left at home in consideration.

Neither dollars nor holsters nor white skin
could save Ted. Neither of us, nor
those Black kids, would ever be Globetrotters.
None of us called it table tennis.
We were all Generals, the game rigged
for the amusement of—of who?
We picked up "equalizers"
and used them to shoot each other instead.

I squeezed the ping-pong ball
gently in my palm like a worry stone
or silver dollar or fake ID.
Mr. C. dropped us off, then drove away
to wherever he lived. At home,
I dropped onto the couch.
Our Christmas lights did not blink.
Look, I said to my parents,
opening my palm:
perfect, round, white.

ABANDONED SCHOOL IN THE RAIN

At the end of the 2007 school year, Jane Cooper Elementary (built in Detroit in 1920) was left unsecured in the middle of the wasteland where a middle-class neighborhood once stood. It took "scrappers" only a few months to strip the building of every last ounce of metal and leave it looking as though it hadn't been occupied for decades.

"School's Out Forever," *Vice*

Rain blew in through busted glass,
shredded blinds flapped then slammed
in wind's erratic rhythm. A sludge of books
mounded on the floor, pages pasted
into a permanent flurry of wilted flowers.
And the papers, and their ink, grades smeared
into a blue-red bruise. Junked computers morphed
into boulders that glaciers of hope left behind.
A spray of white barbed wire scrawled across
the blackboard, one permanent lesson.
I who have not worshipped here have no sermon.
I imagine a child's song slowed to dirge, waving
a hand in the air, believing in the answer.
Open any book to read the story of rain.

STILL LIFE WITH PHONE BOOTH

Upright coffin of human odors. Hopeless ash of stale smoke. Metallic moist panic. Dried spit and blood on scratched plexiglass. Emotion emergency. Muffle and echo and clank of receiver dangled. Impenetrable steel cord spooled so you cannot cut it, walk away and talk to God. Come pick me up. Accident. Beat up. Abandoned. Need. Nothing casual about phone-booth words. Anyone watching? Anyone waiting? Any air left? Can I help you? They cannot help you. Operator in a safe dry room with a bag of Fritos and a Coke. Family photos. Inspirational sayings and pictures of pets. Cars slosh through puddles, blurring the world, rain rattling off the public cage. Where to begin? Where to end? Whose numbers are memorized and why? Hers stuck in there, maybe scratched with a key. What would she say now if you called? *Funny, I've been thinking of you?* Would she hang up? Laugh? Could you warm cold wet hands around her voice? Start your car with it? Drive across three states, pull up out front and announce, *I'm back?* Close your eyes and press your head to the greasy smear of someone else's head. You have one minute left, you have 5 seconds, 4, 3, 2, 1. How can I help you? How can you help me? Where to begin in that false light, true darkness? Coins tremble on the metal tray. Insert to continue. Buy more time for bewildered anguish. Tell me about your sins, and I'll tell you about my penance. The empty coin return. The clawing fingers.

PHONE BOOTH, EIGHT MILE AND RYAN

Outside Top Hat, a White Castle knockoff
open 24/7, warm inside, cold out here, eight lanes
of midnight blurring past, slushing into ice,
and you with the hunger of habit
that can't stomach cheap burgers, stepped-
on drugs, arbitrary inflation, manufactured
shortages, threats not idle, Top Hat always
hiring, greasy exhaust of hamburger, exhaust
of idling cars, exhausted resources, exhaustion
without drugs, exhausted by the search
on Eight Mile, sirens passing toward skids,
black-ice midnight, loaded salt trucks
arriving late, you dial and dial
for a lucky number, on the other end
the busy signal of nobody home,
in Top Hat windows, a shooting
gallery of drunks watching you,
watching the siren-blur, or just
doing the Eight Mile stare, exploring
options, making bad coffee last,
you wave to no one, your tank
on empty once again and always,
the bookends of a phone book
dangling empty on a chain
and you keep repeating *I'm good*,
I'll be good, in lieu of a voice
on the other end, your voice
chanting a present and future
fortune depending on what
god you're praying to
in the phone booth
at Eight and Ryan
cold hands cupped against air
hissing through bullet holes.

GOOGLE MAPS: STREET VIEW

Fifteen years ago, I pulled my car to the curb
next to the manhole cover in front of our house
for the last time. For forty years, I'd deposited
small stones, big secrets, and my own spit
for good measure, down into those blind eyes.

I'm rounding off—everything else, recorded history.
From a rainy day thousands of miles away, I google
back those long grey cement slabs, the flat grid,
for a virtual walk around the block: rusted railing
my father installed, check. Pine tree stolen from
Up North, check. Creosoted streetlight pole, check.

I recite the names—dead or gone, down the block.
3-bedroom ranches from the smudged map of the 50s.
The driveway still rivered with my father's
tar streams when he tired of concrete crack filler
that never lasted through winter's fierce blasts.

Lawns half-brown, trees in leaf. Click. Click.
Bored already, fatigued by mirages of emotion
on what looks like one of world's dullest streets.
Still, our reluctant anchors scraped as we drove
away to condos, senior living, cemeteries.

Close your eyes and imagine: young girls playing
cheerleader, none of them rich or smart or dumb enough
to make the cut, or already smoking in the parking lot,
mocking the tryouts. Boys gathered on bikes, hooting
and—I've already forgotten the sounds we made,

the punctuation of curses. Nothing stopped the wind,
not parked cars or dead trees or sirens. But I know who
is left behind those closed doors where I might knock
and be recognized. Down to two: The Kloceks, garage
packed with junk to burden surviving children,

and Mr. Mazorak, so tiny and mean, no one's sure
he's still in there. Perhaps he's dug out and escaped
with what he believes are family secrets: bastard Ricky,
gay Roger, pregnant Renee. I'm worrying these houses
down to nubs, seeing them online, through the distorted

lens of the passing camera. Cloudy. They got that right.
Follow me as we turn the corner in front of the old
Ernst house onto Bach across from the old Kiski place,
and you will see a young Black kid on a bicycle
too small for him. He wears a long white T-shirt,

sweatshirt slung over one shoulder. He looks
straight at the camera. The only person visible
on the entire block. A Black kid where no Black kids
wandered, even lost. Their rigged compasses
never allowed them here. The abstract *them*, concrete

less than a mile away across Eight Mile, the reason
for the early flyers of 70s White Flight further out
into outer-burbia. I'm gone, so I can't tell what he's
in the middle of saying, a slight blur in his features,
but he looks at home, casual smile in the bike seat

of someone who knows where he's going.
He doesn't know me from the impassive eyes
of the manhole cover, the anonymous camera
roving, robotic, leeching memory from cement.
Are you lost? he might be asking. *Can I help you?*

3

GUN/SHY

GUN/SHY

Fact: *The 40 oz. is a hard-hitting, piss-yellow, oblong bottle of 5% ABV malt liquor that gets warm before you even hit the bottom of the glass.*

Fact: *It embodies every aspect of American life: cheap pleasure without the hard work.*

Hypothesis: *The 40 is the most patriotic drink in America.*

Nothing says America like an ice-cold can of mass-produced beer. Anheuser-Busch announced today that the company is replacing the Budweiser logo with "America" on its 12-oz. cans and bottles this summer.

Gun-shy—I've always been more
than a little, even before I got one
shoved in my face up close and personal

behind a liquor store cash register
in Warren on the Detroit border.
Age 16, I was working on getting laid,
shy until drunk, then subtle as a gun.

■■■

When Roy Tubbs down the street still went
to school, sometimes we shared a joint
on the way—a smile-and-a-joke kind of guy,
that early, and stoned.

After he shot his father, I wanted to ask him
why, but never saw him again, though his father
returned to fertilizing lawns with his red truck—

not shy about missing three fingers
on the hand he'd raised against dying.

■■■

The first two people I knew who got shot
got shot by family, both on our block—the other
a kid with my last name who lived across
the street from Tubbs and two doors down.

On a snow day from school, he shot
his little sister, no one to call timeout
to referee or even shovel. The ambulance
spun out, got stuck. We emerged to pelt it
with snowballs, like we did to cop cars,
though, once better informed,
we pushed it out of the ruts.

■■■

School figures in this too, as in, at least
graduate before you ruin your life.
But patience was not the name
of any of our gangs or drugs
or sports teams.

Unrelated to the Black guy with a gun
looking for quick cash, I was not
shot in the store that day. I mention
Black because we were all white
on our block, indiscriminate
with grudges and guns.

■■■

My distant lunar cousin
on a field trip from Detroit for cash
left a can of Colt .45 on the counter—
a jokester side of him he did not reveal
while waving his gun and raising his voice

in an impolite way. The can sweat
a wet circle onto the counter.

Colt's horseshoe logo, and a bucking
horse to suggest the alcoholic kick
of malt liquor, high on the arms list.

Their slogan *it works every time*
is subject to a range of interpretation
of the approximate size of a bullet hole.
Solve referent for *it*.

The Houston Colt .45s baseball team
sported a large gun on their uniforms
till they became the Astros and moved
indoors to get out of the heat. Thus,
the great invention of plastic grass.
I salute them with a can of America.

∎∎∎

The Washington Bullets are gone,
but not the Houston Rockets. No sign
of the Hand Grenades, Bazookas,
or Nuclear Bombs, but the Axe Murderers
have a long tradition on their side.

The police arrived from the white side
of 8 Mile and spat slurs at the scene, loitering
in the ancient air-conditioning racket
of that tiny store crammed with liquor.
They told us they would not solve the crime
due to our proximity to 8 Mile and their
inability to tell one Black man from another.

Alive, and inordinately proud I had not
peed my pants, I mentally embellished
the story to tell my girlfriend Paula after work
with whom *it* was almost *working*.
My boss was inordinately proud of me

for not caving in and handing over
the twenties and checks hidden
in an empty cigarette carton.

I'm looking for another place to use
inordinately. Perhaps Mr. Tubbs
was inordinately proud that his son
had not killed him. Roy had good dope
but moved on to better dope
that made him a little edgy when
Mother Hubbard's cupboard was bare.

His mother was hidden in an empty
cigarette carton somewhere. How
Mr. Tubbs got custody was beyond
the toxic limits of our lawn-fertilized
imaginations. We had an affinity for poison,
where Patience was not a brand of condoms,
much less a virtue. Virtue was a cigarette brand.
Menthol or regular, filtered or unfiltered, though
Marlboro hard pack was our big seller.

I don't own a gun, but I'm related
to white people who do. Police cars
have cameras now. Warren cops haven't
killed any unarmed Black men.
As far as I know. My wallet
is full of qualifications.

■■■

Matches were free. I checked IDs,
though not legal myself. I dreamed
of my name in neon, not on wanted posters,
but we never told each other our dreams,
so it didn't much matter either way.
Colt .45 tasted like shit, even when guzzled

out of quart bottles. My favorite combo:
a quart of Colt and a bottle of Ripple.
A kind of surf and turf or barf and scarf
for the sophisticated teenage set
inordinately fond of puking

then moving on. No big deal—
just the service charge for the buzz.
I never guzzled Colt .45 again
after the robbery. They recovered
no fingerprints, and I recovered
my bravado with Paula
who smoked True Blues

and knew a special occasion
when it hit us over the head
with a gun handle so we culminated
our relationship that night
in the damp grass of her parents' yard
behind the blow-up kiddy pool
using a condom handed down
by my older brother—the traditional
Trojan, which was better than
pulling out, a reckless maneuver
that did not work with her next
boyfriend Laffy Stinkbomb.

His first name *was* Laffy.
Stinkbomb, just a term of affection.
Their kid could be 45 by now.
I don't think they named him Laffy Junior.
I was happy Laffy Senior did not have
a gun, given his jealous nature.

It's like politics, I tried to explain one day
as he choked me against my locker

after Auto Shop. On the other hand,
Danny Krudbum, who I pinned in 15 seconds
in the gym class wrestling tournament,
had a gun, and went on to shoot a business associate
in a start-up drug operation and dump his body
in a snow bank at the junior high.

I could still put someone in a cross-face cradle
if circumstances warranted, though I suspect
if Danny is out of prison and looking for me
he wouldn't wait for the sadistic gym teacher
to blow the whistle. Sadistic gym teachers
were a dime a dozen back then, which must
make them a dollar a dozen, given inflation
and more sophisticated recreational facilities.

I had a chance to buy a handgun
out of the trunk of Matt Schmitt's Plymouth Fury
in the parking lot by the abandoned tennis
court behind Shaw Park-let, but it was like
with the prostitutes we gave a jump to
outside the Top Hat at 3 a.m. one Christmas Eve,
who, given the holiday spirit, offered to go
down on us for free.

Both Matt and the hookers were cheerful
enough about my cowardice, or,
as I call it now, my judiciousness.
I had this crazy idea being a Daniels
on Rome Street meant I should have a gun
in case somebody mistook me for the other guy
whose name, no shit, was Tim, just one letter off.

My whole life, I've been one letter off, for better,
for worse. You might be able to take it out
before you come, but once you pull the trigger,

there's no reverse. And if I sound particularly full
of shit, just remember *it works every time.*

Over forty years ago, on the spot
where that store still stands, I followed
the firefly of a gun waving through the store
in mad hysterical panic while the kid—not
much older than me—used an inordinate number
of variations on the word *fuck*, given
the brevity of our conversation. If *fuck*

is the bullet of words, I'll take the word
itself every time. Chaldeans own the store
now—Christian Arabs, a concept a lot
of those who drink America don't quite get.
I admire the computerized cash register
and bulletproof revolving counter. 99%
of Detroit party stores are owned by Chaldeans.
The other 1% by members of the Patience MC.

∎∎∎

When we were kids—me and Laffy
and the rest—the Canadian TV station
out of Windsor broadcast limbo contests
right after *Popeye* each weekday night.
In Canada, they set the bar lower,
since a gun would just get in the way
of doing the limbo, while in Detroit,
the wobbly bar for peace and justice
was as low as it could go, and people
still tripped over it.

∎∎∎

Despite slander to the contrary, we were
pretty good at shooting each other up back
in the old neighborhood after the '67 uprising

when we got guns to protect us from imaginary
gangs of Black kids gathering on the other side
of 8 Mile. We were stupid enough
to believe we had something they wanted
while we worked at the same factories
made the same money and drove the same
damn cars we all helped build.

It didn't take much to make me gun-shy
for life, but that doesn't mean we shouldn't
have had a powwow down on 8 Mile
where some people with charts and not a whole lot
of patience drew lines on maps that went far afield
from 8 Mile with a bunch of Xs to show us
where all the money was really buried
so that if we could all agree on taking turns shoveling,
we might dig up something somewhere to share.

■■■

Is giving a jump to a couple stranded hookers
in the Top Hat parking lot the best thing I ever did?
Or, are they the ones who gave us a jump?

Roy Tubbs and his father never seemed shy
to me. In daylight, always ready to give you
a smile beneath their sunglasses,
as if you knew something and they knew
something and the rest of the world beyond
Rome Street didn't have a clue.

Roy's sister Marlene offered me
her virginity one sober afternoon
in their dark empty house. I wasn't sure
I was going to mention Marlene at all—
hers was my first funeral and she, my first kiss—
it seems like too much for this story packed
with lies, overlapping with lies, like the narrow

brick houses on our narrower streets.
Marlene, 14, showed me her father's guns
and offered me lemonade, homemade
with one of those frozen cans you emptied
out and added a can of water to.

We made up a lot of our own definitions
and nicknames, bored with lighting up
those free packs of matches and tossing them
in the street where they burned out. If the guy
had shot me for not giving up our hiding place,
I wouldn't have gotten laid that night
though maybe someone would have lit
a candle for me in church before heading out
to the parking lot to light up the Truth.

I can't remember everything
but I do not have to, being white.
Maybe I offered my virginity to Marlene?

■■■

If we'd had a powwow on 8 Mile
maybe I would've run into my Black relative
adopted specifically for this poem
and he could have told me what
a patronizing motherfucker I was,
and we could have shaken hands
and said, *Hard feelings*, and been honest
on that unforgiving road.

■■■

Growing up, we had no protection
from guns or story problems.
The math nearly killed us all.
Being white, I can joke about it:
sex and guns. The other Daniels
shooting his sister. They did not

catch the robber with the gun.
Maybe he's out there wearing
a throwback Colt .45 jersey
for old-timers night.

The kid shouted at me
where's your fucking hiding place
because all white people
have hiding places, even while making
less than minimum wage at a corner store
on the edge of Detroit. It's a luxury we have,
and he was out to collect luxury tax.

I still burned with hot-sweat anger and fear.
That's how it's supposed to work: hating
on each other over nickels and dimes
when we're all in the same damn zip code,
area code, the same class, the same teachers
flunking us on exams for Patience and Virtue.
The rust on our automobiles
the same color. I have no authority,
having stabbed myself
with my fake badge. Fake guns
aren't so fake anymore.

■■■

For much of my life
I've resisted parking
between the yellow lines,
but not all of my life,

my life, my life. Sixty
years, and I've never
felt like I might be shot
again. At sixty,
still allowed to be shy
in all this white space.

4

LEAVING THE PIANO BEHIND

FISHING IN THE CEMENT POND

Schenley Park, Pittsburgh

Most people don't even know about the pond
at the bottom of the deep hollow, reached
only by an ancient staircase crumbling down
the hillside. We slid down on our asses
with our plastic poles and can of worms dug
from our yard's packed dirt. My son, six,
the pond enormous in his squint.

Under the shadow of the high bridge, among
crushed appliances and bald tires, green glass shards
and disintegrating cardboard, we sat on the pond's
cement lip—man-made and man-ruined,
yet fat, wizened catfish, murky shadows of carp,
wallowed. Flimsy bluegill shimmered with illusion.
He wanted to keep his first. It swallowed the hook.

I wiggled it out, returned the fish to water,
but it floated back toward us through the murk.
We could almost see our house above the hillside,
but my son was glad we couldn't. We saw a large man
on a milk crate fishing as if he cared. My son wanted to row
across on a raft of tires or in a fridge with the door removed.

Above us, the city passed another hot, endless August day.
Traffic from the freeway hissed through trees.
Our dead fish shone flat in the sun. The blind fisherman
flinched at our casting. He asked my son to tell him
what he saw, and was told a tale of gigantic proportions.
The man cocked his head and laughed. *I do believe
I hear the waves*, he said. The cement pond—
giant sea shell or rusted car—magnified all sound.

We ran out of worms or the fish stopped biting.
A thin line of sweat glistened on my son's upper lip.
He'd caught his first fish and talked to a blind man.

The city waited above us with red signs and yellow lines.
Can we get lost on the way home? he asked. You need
a map for that, I said. We struggled up the broken steps.
How did the man get down there? he asked.
The sea was vast and unknowable.

STRAWBERRIES AND MIRRORS

We live on the same planet
as strawberries and mirrors, smoke
and breath, minor sin and major celebration.
Is an apple really that tempting,

even when glossed by a serpent's skin?
In all the stories, it's an apple—
as if betrayal needs such sturdy fruit.
What about the slipperiness of sin?

A strawberry from my garden,
smaller than supermarket size—
but with a red that sucks in sun,
spins it into rich glow and melts

in tender, sweet collapse inside
your mouth—is more like it.
My children adore strawberries
bordering on sin, to be confessed,

if that was a box we checked
on the sin-meister's list.
Our hallway mirror evidenced
by smudges as they check out

how they will be checked out
when they smile like this,
dance like this, when they break
down the gates of hell like this.

A rule against me watching, though
I pass that tollbooth a dozen times a day,
and they spend enough time there
to be accruing pension benefits.

All the snake dude needed to do
was stick a mirror tree in Eden

to stop traffic to eternal happiness.
If Adam and Eve were teenagers

they'd be out sucking icicles
and bitching about the furnace
before God could even lock
the gate behind them.

The steam off a living thing is my idea
of heaven, though how much does
a doubter's vote count? Clouds of it rise
off my children today, waiting for the bus,

refusing all my designations for them
as they stand between the strawberry and the mirror,
the serpent coiling and uncoiling in the steam,
like God's smile as he jingles his keys, says,

have a nice day.

MY DAUGHTER TURNED THIRTEEN TODAY

The sky turned to ash above her.
The cement mumbled into dust
below. Her father stood waving
his arms in front of God's window.

My daughter turned thirteen today
and the wisdom of flying any flag
turned dubious, and the night trembled
in its thin dress and moaned.

My daughter turned thirteen today
and the moon had no comment
and the radio signals from the star molecule
of her birth returned in frenzied static.

My daughter turned thirteen today
and songs were sung by hibernating insects
and large women with time on their hands
and stout men in silly uniforms
and dogs with attitude.

My daughter turned thirteen today
and gave me a face I have already forgiven,
for I turned thirteen once and spun
on the dime's face and swore to live
forever even if it killed me
and I am still here puzzling it out.

My daughter turned thirteen today—
nothing cute about it. *Remember when
we used to hold hands?* She erased
that memory with the very hand I held.

My daughter turned thirteen today
and the paperwork got lost in the mail.
My daughter turned thirteen today
and I worried the sliver in deep.

I hold the closed eyes of her first dream
against the swallowed clock's brief satisfaction.
Night lights click off. Love is patient in its
delicate skin woven from scaffolding past.
I welcome its brief mirage. Thirteen, today.

PRIVATE ROOM

My daughter got sick and nearly died—
fall of ninth grade. She combed her hair out.
I kissed her goodbye and goodnight

each time I left, and she had no choice,
attached to grim tubes, prone, ashen.
My daughter sick and nearly dying

of embarrassment as doctors probed
the mystery and fought among themselves.
I missed her goodbyes and goodnights.

We watched an old movie from child-
hood. No game shows or reality. Fourteen.
My daughter. Sick with worry she

would die, I slept on the floor and wept.
I pressed heat packs against her to stop tremors,
then kissed her, since I could. Goodnight

seemed insufficient. So did I. No curfew
in that moonless room without boys.
My daughter got sick. Death passed her by—
I snuck her home. We did not kiss. Goodnight.

TEST BOMB FALLOUT

Too young to drive ourselves, we dropped our paper-
stuffed dummy strung over the streetlight onto passing cars.
A matter of timing, knowing when to let go.

Life was a prank no one had pulled on us yet.
Every month, a moon emerged from night's starry hat.
We tossed the winking dummy over the streetlight

like mad puppeteers, hoarse ventriloquists of night. The pulse
of burning strummed through the heavy rope released
by three boys, giddy with the matter of timing, eager to let go.

Cars braked, to our delight. We ran or stayed, depending
on who emerged, what shade the relieved blossom of rage.
We dropped a homemade bomb off the streetlight until

police whirled red and cuffed the dummy. Whose clothes
did it wear, whose cap, whose grin? God's grainy photo
in dim night's news. We had no paper trail. How to let go?

When our friend fell to earth, did not land, drilled right through,
we hung our heads like failed firemen among ashes. The silence
of a body swaying beneath a streetlight—abandoned dummy
who thought it did not matter if time stopped, if he let go.

POISON CONTROL

for Chuck

Thirsty from cutting grass,
you drank weed killer
thinking it was lemonade.
Why did we believe this?

Fifteen years old, class president.
No room on our crowded concrete
for the silver sliver of suicide,
nail puncturing tire forever.

■ ■ ■

My daughter once believed
if she stopped doing some bad thing
and started walking backward,
we could not see her.

My son, fourteen, cut himself twice.
Once with the jackknife his uncle
gave him. Once with scissors.
We hid the kitchen knives, the pills.

The toxic cleansers, solutions, polishers.
We hid it all so well that even now
I cannot find my X-acto knife.
Not too deep. Not clear why.

Each tentative slice some odd notch
of being fourteen, untranslatable
unhappiness, his body shooting up
beyond mine into thin air he choked on.

Treasure trove of ways not to hurt yourself
buried without a map. He wandered, refusing

our tainted directions. What could we offer
for him to grip as tight as a knife?

■■■

Chuck—never Charlie—started walking
backward on us, and we stopped
seeing him, just tightened our street-corner
circle and went on cracking dirty jokes

putting each other down, pretending
we liked cigarettes. Hell of a grass cutter,
that Charles. Good at math too. Taste buds
unrefined. Yeah, let's put weed killer

in a jug so it looks like lemonade.
Alone at his grandparents' cottage
when they found him. I don't buy
the story now, and I don't accept
bribes to take it either.

■■■

My son alone in his room.
We have to knock. He talks to
a counselor. My kids heard me swear
for the first time when the guy

wouldn't take our insurance.
Fuck, I hissed. I tremble. I press
my fingers against his cold door
and listen for his breath.

■■■

I rattled a bottle of blue pills
in view of my ex-girlfriend
imagining the music might bring her
back, but she played the piano—

I had almost forgotten that—sweet notes
drowning my lame percussion, tears lulling
me back into a world with tickets for future
heartbreak, but a world nonetheless.

∎∎∎

The first president to die in office.
Who remembers Chuck now,
his small spurt of life evaporated?
His parents. We rattle our pill bottles

at each other across the distance—
louder, for we are losing our hearing.
We are walking backward
rendering ourselves invisible.

∎∎∎

My son and I take the same antidepressants.
Is that depressing, or what? Fuck. We are part
of the U.S. Maraca Band. We play at weddings,
not funerals. Chuck's parents called it a tragic

accident. We called it a tragic accident.
We went on taming lawns with sharp
blades and continue to this day. We
who never quenched such thirst.

MUSIC OF THE LIGHT TIMER

Still light steady in the dark silent house.
My daughter played piano for five years,
then stopped. My son learned to blow
one clear note on the saxophone,
then stopped. Its black case sat mocking
till we gave it to our friends' son
who also abandoned it.

He had ambitions, the other boy,
of becoming a pro wrestler. My son
wanted to be a professional lip-syncher.
My daughter wanted to be a ballerina vampire
princess, and one Halloween she was.

Me? I mostly wanted to get stoned,
and mostly did until I stopped. And stopped.
And stopped again. If we graphed our failures,
if we broke our crayons and went on strike,
if we danced in somebody's perpetually
dim basement, then what?

I left home for the last time at 25,
after detoxing. I helped my mother decorate
the Christmas tree, both of us framed
in firm steady light through the front window
of our dull house on the sharp edge of Detroit.

Tonight, the still steady house in Pittsburgh's
dark light, my children charting high
on their separate angular paths
away from me, well above my jagged spikes.

Winter—I keep adding layers against the cold.
The other boy drowned last year, and our friends
continue to drown this year. My children
are not coming home. Yes, silence—
the instrument I am learning to play at last.

LEAVING THE PIANO BEHIND

We packed the shrunken sleep of old pillows and the broken wedding clock. We packed the frazzled mop and the shaved head of the basketball. We packed the love letters of the insane yellowing in a box. We packed three trophies, one for each sport, and discarded the others. We packed the extra wine glasses that would be extra forever since I swore off the stuff. I swore I wouldn't take so much stuff, but I packed the winter socks from my Dad's dead friend Mac and the sport coat my son outgrew. We packed my daughter's IV port and my son's pre-surgery video. We packed sour dreams stale dreams overcooked still-raw dreams—all the dreams came along and most of our broken sunglasses. We dumped random drawers into boxes and marked them *fragile*. The whoosh of thirty years, the chill of newly empty rooms, the choked-back tears, even the worn welcome mat on our way out the door, but we left the piano upright in the corner, having taken all its songs, having loved its silence, having watched our children's fingers dully press the keys, having survived the lost names, the floods of grief, the midnight phone calls, the joyful dancing, the joyful phone calls, the midnight dancing. We left the piano movers suspended in comic waiting. We left the piano in the mute awe of our lives lived there. We left the piano untunable, humming goodbye or hello, one long held note.

HALE BOPP

Our children were two and three,
and the soft, wobbly anchors of their hands
held ours, down the dirt road past
the bare, stitched grapevines of winter—
before green eruptions, before the calm,
round glow of fruit—to the village for bread,
warm bread, softening between their new teeth.
My daughter, two, squinted up at us, grinning,
with a handful and mouthful.

We threw an anchor off the boat
of our new life as a family, dragged it
behind us to plow up the fields
of our fallow hearts. The name of God
came unbidden to our lips, and that
was enough—to say the name,
not worship or confess.

■■■

I had never seen a sky rubbed that clean
and smooth, polished into forever—blue,
then black, black, then blue, while we threw
sticks in a stream to watch them float away
and anchored ourselves against fierce wind.

When the comet appeared, we did not try
to measure or weigh it, explain or worship it.
It was enough to look up into clear sharp night
and nod to the long streaming tail
like the high linger of a tiny bell, a graceful spill
of gold grains onto fine grass, not driven or ridden
not occupied or domesticated. Could sleeping horses
smell the rosemary of it?

Our children called it *the spilled stars*—
spills a part of our days, plates and glass
shattering on stone floors, slipped

from their tiny grips. Spilled stars
that no one erased or wiped up or swept away.

In the tiny village church, a large choir sang
and a pig joyfully wallowed in mud next door.
I killed a rat chewing a nest in the spare bed
with a thick book of lullabies. A farm rat
that meant no harm, but I'd been spiked
by fear. The children slept through it.
We unwrapped the gifts of their futures
as if we had control. Hunks of fresh bread
glowing in our fists.

Live in a place long enough, and you'll need
new shoes, or at least a haircut. Do not count
your blessings. Sprinkle your blessings
like star-spill on those you love.
And if I am talking out of turn,
like I know a thing or two, forgive me.
Four of us eased down the narrow path
to the bread we called communion.

We shouldn't have gone back, but we did
ten years later. Bored in Paradise, our son
watched TV on his iPod and our daughter
watched an old German series about a dog
on the tiny set in our room with a view.

Does belief in God mean that we believe
we won't want to come back?
Every anchor temporary, and flight
impossible. The comet, a dream now,
erased from the skies of this thin bright city.

Once we lay for hours in a field of wildflowers
dimmed by night. Our children slept
on our chests—warm breath, calm rise
and fall, as we stared up at the comet.

It did not damage our sight or cut the rope
for us, who worship falling. It did not
abandon us into weeping.

We should not map our lives,
but we do: the bright smudge
of my finger pointing upward
as if I believed. The sprinkle
of trailing stars.

5

THE GRAND DESIGN

MY MOTHER ADVISES ME
TO GET A MANI/PEDI

The last few days in the hospital
were—she hesitates—it sounds
crazy, she knows—a nice change
of pace—not *nice*, she says, but . . .

89, blind, behind the unsteady anchor
of her walker, she drifts, rope frayed,
Depends afloat like abandoned life vests.
On the phone hundreds of miles away—

she pushes *mute* by mistake. I call again.
Busy. She curses unseen buttons.
We got her a phone she can shout
our names into. How many times

did she shout *Call Jim* today?
In the hospital they chipped off
her nail polish for the ET monitor
that pulses her finger aglow.

She gets them painted bright
as ambulance lights. Sirens.
My sister will take her out today
to get them redone. I'm stressing

over workplace betrayals, reckless kites
of my children, insomnia crows hovering
over the headboard like they did for her
for years until the pills kicked their asses.

Mani/Pedi, she says. Most days, no one
touches her. Not my father, studying maps
of places he'll never find again. It's not all
sadness and fake moonlight. Some days

there's the hospital and more tests.
Dead leaves skitter over the sidewalk here

where I'm at. *Stress*, she says, *I hear it
in your voice. They massage your feet.*

It feels so good. She sees distorted blurs
of color, and hallucinations she can some-
times still identify as such. *They were nice
to me in the hospital. The food was better.*

What they eat at home—we've all gone over
it, and her guardian angel is no help.
It feels so good.
                 I'm sure it does, I say,

but she's pushed *mute* again. Then briefly back:
CALL JIM, she shouts, then gone again. On repeat,
though there's no button for that. I don't call her
back again. Nothing more to say right now.

The Wound Doctor

drilled through
to the bone
to dig out the pus.

    I'm blaring "One Monkey
    Don't Stop No Show" by Joe Tex
    loud enough to let me scream the lyrics.

My father's bone. 89.
Wounded playing softball.
Don't laugh like the wound doctor did
at the old man who will never field
a grounder again and, at 89, does not
want to manage instead. He is tired

    of managing. My blind mother cannot watch
    him play and he can only leave her alone
        so long
        so long softball:

the uniform
the glove
the magic bat.

    All his friends have died except Lenny
    and he's in Phoenix
    and not rising.

Burying season almost over:
Lenny's wife, Mac's wife, then Mac—
drinking again after forty years sober
found on the floor surrounded
by beer cans, his first crush.

    The wound nurse arrives each day
    to repack it, as if the wound can't decide
    whether or not to take the trip.

She fills it with goop as if measuring
an ingredient for a boring recipe.

    My mother can't drive
    my father can't drive
    both stiff with deafness
    TV so loud neither of them
    wakes as I enter the light

from the darkness of a long drive across three states
to do what? One monkey. One wound. STOP.

    New skin will fill the hole
    if he waits and lives long enough.

Don't laugh. Don't cry. This is the sad part
that churns like watery gas in the heart's engine—
so, I'm speeding through the blur of Detroit lights
off the freeway—my mother said my father could
not sleep, hobbling through the house, lost dog
rabid with worry, so finally she made room
in her single bed, and he curled beside her.

I don't have enough space to leave here
        for that.
They're stealing each other's walkers
by accident
        by accident
ground ball foul from the next field over.

I packed a toothbrush and my own pills
and the pair of warm socks Mac gave me
when he retired to Arizona—lucky Mac-socks
to keep me from drinking. And screw him

    for starting again and leaving my father
    with Lenny who still thinks he's selling ice cream

to party store owners in Dearborn
through computer magic and secret ice tunnels.

The wound doctor's used to gun shots—an old man
with a softball wound? He can't help himself. He laughs.
No one can help themselves, and that's the damn wound,
excuse me, Doc.

I turn the volume down, and, still,
they do not stir in their special chairs.
My father's magic wireless speaker
perched on the stool beside him.

One monkey, I sing, almost tender.
I do a twist and swivel on the stained rug
in front of them. *Everybody now.*

HIGH SCHOOL DIPLOMA, 1917

Marie Cogan, my grandmother, lost
two children within two years. Balancing
on a wobbly footstool imported from Ireland,
she scrubbed her walls clean of them, then never
cleaned again. Marie Cogan lied about her age
until the past hazed over into truth. The remaining child
conceded to the ghosts, left home and became
my father. Marie Cogan brushed my sister's hair
with the violence of a true believer and took communion
for superstitious reasons. Marie Cogan played cards
with neighbor ladies and collected music boxes,
though eventually lost her false teeth and believed
I was a doctor come to save her. She took her diploma
to the home where it hung above her bed, alone
without photographs: *Marie Cogan*, in stately scrawl
enlarged by pride—few girls finished. Not one careless
scrap of her dead children in the stinging white
of her tiny shared room lit by music boxes
and the stench of dying. My grandfather, entering late
through the back door of their rotting wood-frame house,
takes off his work shoes and hat, washes up at the sink,
and heads to his own cold room in the back. He quit school
to work at Packard's, lying about his age, then had to lie
again, pretending to take the day off to sign up for the draft—
the only lies he ever told, except the ones of omission,
as far as I know, I, who carried both their caskets
and laid them into the earth next to the graves
of those two children, brushing away dirt from flat stones
carved with the names never spoken except haltingly,
once, by my father. *Marie Cogan*, the priest intoned.
She lived her whole life in one house until she could
no longer. *Marie Cogan*. I will sing her name
in the Old English script. Holy Redeemer High School,
have mercy on us all.

DECLARING BANKRUPTCY

On the phone with Logan, nostalgia's
inflationary tendencies hit me upside
the head. He's at his mother's—
she who angrily remembers nothing.
Tell her I said hi hi hi.
He's lost his business and maybe

it's not my business, but I call
from three states away, offer condolences,
etc.—it's all in the silences. He's shrugging
it off, though I can't see the shrugs.
I hear the wistful drift, the shame of not
getting the joke, wrong end of the telescope,

rain blowing through the screen to warp
the floorboards—that kind of storm.
When I was sick for the forever
of six childhood weeks, he knocked softly
on the door, and we built houses of cards
in the warm silence of the late afternoon rug.

See what I mean about nostalgia?
We start talking at the same time,
then both stop and wait. What do you do
at age 58 when you lose your business
after 32 years? No cake, no candles.
300 miles away, I listen to the same rain.

Giving up the ghost. Looking for another
ghost. He's buried his father, his daughter,
his partner in the bar. So who am I to offer
condolences now? Two photos: 1) in Eagles
uniforms, gloves at our feet 2) in tuxedos
in the street before we pick up prom dates.

Luxury tax on nostalgia. Storm's not letting
up. Looks like a rainout. Looks like
Monopoly in the basement, farting contests

and Kool-Aid—I could go on forever,
but I'll leave us naked, streaking through
Big Boy's on Eight Mile—who were

those crazy kids? You had to have been there
and we were, having given up all our assets,
having revealed all our assets. Get it? No joke.
Monopoly in the basement
        wrong end of the telescope
          wistful drift

that kind of storm
        say hi to your mother
            tell her I remember everything.

FIRST WEEK BACK AFTER STENT

Friday afternoon. When it's this gray,
Canadians emerge to turn *a* to *e*: Grey Friday.
My light bulb glows like Miss Mousey's
moon. Wristwatches twitch like whiskers.
Workday math, solve for zero.
The light bulb in my desk lamp reflects
off the office window and reminds me
of my old friend's flashlight in a musty tent
fifty-some years ago and counting
on the fingers of our shadow puppets.

■■■

In the building across the way, a woman
folds clothes. I itch where they shaved
my chest. Too cold for her to step
naked onto her balcony and wave,
though I imagine it anyway:
Hey old guy! Get a load of this!
I don't need the Whole Shebang.
Give me half the Shebang. We can split it.
We can exchange it for other people's Shebang.
I once went for the Whole Shebang
and came back with a bootleg tattoo
of Jesus Christ's signature. Imagine
my surprise. Imagine my chagrin.
I take Chagrin with my coffee. Half
a teaspoon. If you have a Chagrin
substitute, I'll take that. Vexation—
yes, that'll be fine.
They dug craters in my chest to grasp
my heart and squeeze. *See, it's still beating*,
they said. Better than a colonoscopy.
No Shebang in that.
I gave up smoking and started building
plastic models of cigarettes—Winston,
Marlboro, Pall Malls, I've got 'em all.
The glue makes it worthwhile.
From here, she looks in the pink,

but I'm in the red, and blue.
Hey, Canadian friend, can you turn
message into massage?
Vitals into vittles?

■■■

What's she doing over there,
ironing my medical reports?
I know a man who became rich
imitating the sound of a time clock.
I'm writing my life sentence
today, Friday afternoon.
My old friend with the flashlight
made finger puppets of every lie
I ever told him. Lies like
we'll be friends forever
and *my parents never have sex.*
Or maybe the light was playing tricks
on me. The moon could explain
a lot of things, but it glows faint
during working hours.
In a minute—can you turn minutes
into manure? Can you fertilize bullshit
or is that redundant? I take Redundant
in my coffee. It keeps me regular—
in a minute, we'll all be marching
to the elevators, singing the Company Song.
I auditioned for marionette—I mean majorette—
but I only got to be a minorette.
But I still remember all the words,
so repeat after me.

ANNUAL CHECKUP WITH MONEY SPECIALIST

I met with the retirement doctor yesterday,
salt-splatter on my jeans from Planet February.
He had on his flamenco youth shirt
and his haircut from Risk University.
He shook my hand, and my hand shook.
I searched for a more difficult target,
but the office was invisible except for
complimentary beverages and candy.
A minty lifesaver burned in my belly.
Dissolving is an abstract concept
until you're just a puddle. This guy's
in his thirties, and he knows everything
just like I did. The retirement doctor
took X-rays of my copies and helped me
put my coat on. What happened in between,
eaten away by salt just doing its job.
My file turned into a series of equal signs
tracked across the page as I drove away.
He told me some jokes about dying
that I will not tell today.

MIRACLES

I'm sorry for praying to God
    to bring a snow plow down my street.

He knows and I know that I'm not one of his guys.
    The Mayor's Hotline wails, busy as a siren.

I confess to cussing out the neighbor on crutches
    who accused me of burying his car in shoveled snow.

When we got the first two feet, people took photos
    of beautiful drifts. Then tree branches cracked

off, downed power lines. Then we tried to shovel.
    Then car after car, stuck, abandoned at mad angles

of the possessed and despondent. My age started
    barking: back, shoulder, elbow.

After the third foot, craven altars to false gods
    arose clumped on street corners.

Weather forecasters erupted in flamboyant orgasms.
    They train hotline workers to be kind and patient.

I think they kidnap ancient grandmothers and feed them
    candy lipstick. This morning I woke

to the blessed rumble of plows gathered on the corner.
    I ran out and waved them down, dancing

on my mountain of piled snow. I would say *as God
is my witness*, but I'm not so sure he's still

around. I left an apology on the neighbor's windshield
    and searched for my own car buried blocks away

where I abandoned it after drunk college students refused
    to help. Sainthood is a long, drawn-out process,

like the death penalty. One guy's miracle is another guy's
    last meal. It's snowing again, or still. They are laying

hands on the giant greenscreen map on TV, evangelists
    for disaster. The snowplows scraped away six days of it.

Will I see another storm like this in my lifetime?
    I trudge out into it—in my lifetime, in my lifetime—

too deep to make an angel without disappearing.

SPANNING

I love bridges, the narrower
the better. So narrow you have
to wait for a car coming the other way,
wave it on so you can be joyful
and generous and wait your turn.
You have to slow down
and not scrape the sides
with your vehicle or psyche,
tenderly gripping the steer-
ing wheel and commenting
on the weather seeping in
through the suddenly musical
windows to whoever might be
listening, and you love whoever
forever, even if they're asleep
in the backseat, slack mouths agape.
You're moving slow enough
to feel the bridge sway, adjust.
Even though you have not risen,
you are now above—almost
hovering, floating, almost flying
over air, water, steep hillsides,
as if God has rolled his magic dice
and called your name, or so you imagine,
so you're hearing, because you've slowed
down and turned careful, and the world
has blanketed your loved ones
in seats around you, and you might see someone—
not a toll taker or inspector or customs official
or uniformed uniform, not someone
with a hand out for documents or payment—
just someone looking up or across or over
or even down from higher ground,
someone who sees you pause on the bridge
(oh the many journeys, the many bridges
you might never cross again), a someone
who offers the generous, unexpected gift
of a hand waving in the air.
You wave back.

THE SECRET AGENT BRIEFCASE

When I got my professor gig, my parents
bought me a narrow hard-sided briefcase
with a combination lock. You could sit on it.
Stand in principle on it. Smack it upside your
head to get your smarts going. You could not
squeeze many books into it. When I pressed
the latches and it clicked open, I expected
to see a bomb. I carried it to school
my first fall until a colleague joked
You got a bomb in there? He called me
the Secret Agent, though I stopped using it
immediately. It sat in my bedroom closet
with slippers I never wore. Thanks,
Mom and Dad. I gave it to Goodwill last week
with a load of my children's outgrown clothes.
Some guy down on his luck might love
that briefcase—to mess with his friends,
to absorb strange looks from downtowners
passing his homeless station. Perhaps he will
fill it with meaningful papers or half-eaten
hamburgers or the holy relics of his tough life.
When I got my gig, two years removed
from the line at Ford's beside my father,
I had a couple bad habits and a trunk full
of good luck, driving from Detroit to Pittsburgh
with enough drugs to last till I found a local dealer.
A new pair of shoes blistered my feet.
The drugs nearly covered the shame
of my blunt speech in that nuanced landscape
of betrayal. No wonder, blisters. No wonder,
the bomb. I used the briefcase years later
as a prop for a movie I made that no one saw,
making it that much more experimental
and noteworthy in my annual report. I carry
my books in a backpack and my shame
in a secret pocket. I have less of it
these days—the old professor, survivor
of fake bomb threats in petty emails.

I was a secret agent after all.
A double agent. An agent who carved
his own decoder ring at weekly meetings
of the special club where the man
with my briefcase might appear
some day, just when I need him.
My parents came to town
when I got my endowed chair.
My blind mother in her green raincoat.
My father in his funeral overcoat.
I myself had purchased a suit.
The hors d'oeuvres were tasteless,
but my father enjoyed the novelty
of stuffed mushrooms, and my mother,
the mini egg rolls. I circled my parents
like a dog protecting its wounded master.
Though who was wounded?
I keep my old factory lunch bucket
in my office at the university,
dull gray scratches, dents
in black paint. I rub it for luck
before meetings of the committee
on screechy chairs. If that seems
like sad nostalgia to you,
perhaps you're right.
But it too is hard.
It too protects what's inside.

HONORARY HONOR

Poet laureate of my neighborhood
until I took out garbage on the wrong day.
For poets, every day is garbage day, I said.
Tell that to the landfill, they said.
They appointed the blind woman across
the street to replace me. She's loud
but polite. Poet laureate of my house
until I forgot to make my bed. I'm just going
to lie in it again anyway, I said. They said
you're sleeping on the job, and appointed
the dog instead. His poems untranslatable,
but he offers protection.
Now, I'm poet laureate of my closet.
Everyone loves me there, alone in the dark.

PROPERTY VALUE

February, when all hope ices over
into treachery. My homeless neighbor
on his back-porch dump slurps soup
magnified off cracked concrete, leafless stubble.
Okay, not homeless—just no water, electricity, heat.
Squatter in his own house? You give it a name.
He's drizzling soup into his beard and squinting
at two junk cars in his yard reflecting winter sun
beside a church organ wrapped in plastic—
he takes all donations. In court, the judge called him
a cancer on the community. You who do not live
next door might sympathize. Even the exterminator
couldn't believe anyone lives there. Next door
for thirty years, I was patient for twenty.
I've got a beard, like him. Two kids, like him,
long gone. Compassion can turn in your gut
like bad meat, and just the sight of it makes you
want to puke. Right, neighbor? He won't look my way.
Not since court. We've failed, both of us,
to finish those songs we were writing to the moon,
but I still have water and heat and light in February.
The social worker has no will. A couple of quiet knocks
on the front door he never uses, and she's gone.
Help is a funny thing, but nobody's laughing
on Ridgeview Avenue in Pittsburgh.
Last words he spoke to me: *Happy Father's Day*
when I passed on the way to lunch with my kids.
That's his idea of—well, you're probably saying
either I have no perspective or I'm a hard,
selfish bastard, and both are true.
But I've got to tell someone about the steam
rising from his soup before it cools.

NEIGHBOR DOWN ON BRIDGE

I spotted a fallen man on the bridge
over Panther Hollow. Had he tumbled askew
to get a better look at the hawk in its nest
in a tree at the edge, or gliding overhead
to raise every hair on his body?
I swerved back across the street
then ran down the sidewalk: my neighbor
whose wife died last year. Exposed, prey,
he'd refused to stop walking, though half-deaf,
three-quarters blind, on dialysis and heart meds.
I yelled my name into his face bloody
from the fall. *I was trying to take a step,*
he said, calmly bewildered, as if starting
an explanation of his entire life, *but it was
all shadow.* I shrugged him up, and we locked
arms like desperate old chums off to see the wizard.
Wind cut through the hollow without mercy
or doubt. He clutched my hand and asked
about my family like what I said might change
the world. I shuffle-stepped him off
to his son's house. Blood ran down his temple.
I had nothing to wipe it with. *Am I bleeding?*
he whispered as I rang the bell. His son took him
from me, as a man takes a child, as I would take
my own father back, swallowing my entire life
to see him that way. If I had a message here,
the hawk has taken it to feather its nest.

EMPTY NEST

I planted a new tree in the yard
where the old one died.
I miss my children away at college.
Because of the old tree.
Because of their attempts
at climbing.
When we bought the house
I thought the dwarf crabapples
of the old tree were cherries.
The children collected them
like rare counterfeit coins.
Sky blue can't be reproduced
in a crayon. Not when sun shines
like today. Not when my kids
hundreds of miles away
have grown taller than me.
I can no longer taste their dreams.
What will the new tree shade—
when and if it grows, fills out—
over the tiny square yard?
Will it thicken with years enough
to climb? With time for research,
I learn you can eat the new tree's
berries. If you beat the birds to them.
The kids' tiny crabapples lay rotting
and counted into neat piles in the grass.
The spindly new tree barely makes
a shadow. Birds on the high wire
not interested in today's news.
No nesting place in this spineless tree.
The birds might be sparrows.
For no apparent reason
they rise into flight.

RIPE SERVICEBERRIES

Squeeze one to check for give. Ripe serviceberries are closer to soft than hard. Each individual berry grows on its own stem . . . no mechanical method exists to harvest the fruit. The work goes faster if you bring along friends.

The birds and I have been waiting
in trees and on back stoops.
I don't know how birds know
the berries are ripe.
Or if trust or sharing
is in the vocabulary of birds.
I don't know if the birds
understand that it's my tree.
I can go on forever
with all I do not know.
But I do know
when they are closer
to soft. *Mine.*

■■■

I know a cedar waxwing
with a plump berry in its beak
is worth the taste of ten berries
in the service of mathematical
equivalencies designed by spring's
white spray of flowers
which leads to this. I want to be
closer to soft than hard.
I want to bring along friends.
I can go on forever
with all I want.

TYING MY SHOE AT THE NEW PORNOGRAPHERS CONCERT

Mr. Smalls Theater

We stood on the deconsecrated concrete floor
of the old church turned nightclub
and got our ears blasted while I searched
for someone my age. Bald guy up front?
Maybe. My wife and I, too late to get a seat
in the choir loft, stood below
with eager boppers and swayers
through an hour of Jail, the warm-up band.
Yes, capital J Jail. Below zero outside.
We waited to get wrist-banded
like endangered birds to be tagged
and released. Have I.D. Available.
No Exceptions. I have not had a drink
since—well, I didn't bother pulling
mine out. Something crude about that
phrase—I'm 59, going on whatever's
next. She made no exceptions, despite
my protest: I won't be at the bar.
She nearly ruffled my white hair
like I was team mascot for the cemetery.
I couldn't quite follow Jail's between-
song patter about video games. I'm losing
my hearing—easier for concerts,
or harder? Jail finished.
My wife and I didn't talk about this
afterwards, but I'm telling you:
I bent down to tie my shoe halfway
through the New Pornographers,
sold-out crowd squeezed body
to body against the altar/stage—
I told her I was going down.
I leaned a hand against her waist
to steady myself. An alarmed
young couple beside us expressed

concern. My wife shouted quickly,
he's okay, he's just dying.
I mean, he's okay, he's just
tying his shoe,
I mean, he's okay, he just
wants to kneel on the floor
and whisper a prayer
like in the old days.

FINAL MIRACLE BEFORE RETIRING FROM SLOWPITCH

My latest prayer consists of nonsense syllables
based on the friction of two sticks rubbing together.
The best kind of nonsense, I've decided, no clever-
ness about it. I prefer people to pat me on the ass
rather than stab me in the back, but I've obtained
good drugs for stab wounds. I can't pronounce
them, but they all contain the prefix or suffix *damn*.
Until recently, I still played softball
and occasionally got a pat on the ass.
Then, at age 60, I got taken out at second base
by a young man with a limited vocabulary.
Rubbing two sticks together requires a certain
patience. And perhaps at least a slight belief
in some higher power. If the guy had just asked,
I'd have said, Sure, you can be safe, dude,
just don't go breaking that rib God took
from Adam and gave to me. Lying
in dirt, trying to catch my breath,
which had a mind of its own, staggering away
into an overcast sky, I could only gasp out
my nonsense. On my hands and knees—
the position for prayer I've finally landed on.
Was my foot on the bag?
Did I hold onto the ball long enough?
I rubbed two ribs together
and burst into flame.

THE GRAND DESIGN

The Millau Viaduct that spans the valley of the river Tarn in Southern France is the tallest bridge in the world. The bridge has been consistently ranked as one of the great engineering achievements of all time.

Legend has it that Roquefort cheese was discovered when a youth, eating his lunch of bread and ewes' milk cheese, saw a beautiful girl in the distance. Abandoning his meal in a nearby cave, he ran to meet her. When he returned a few months later, the mold had transformed his plain cheese into Roquefort.

How many times have you had the time of your life?
I just had shoulder surgery so I could play softball again.
Does that make me a seventh-day resurrectionist?
What would Jesus do? He would've had the surgery.

My wife and I . . . are you bored already?
The moon and the mad pencil sharpener—
is that better? The happy moon sharpener
and his gardener sidekick, Hedgeclipper.

Take one for pain. Take two for no pain. Take three
and call me in mourning. Hike. Call me now
and skip the middle part. My wife and I visited
the tallest bridge in the world on the way

to visit the Roquefort cheese caves in France.
The sound-and-light show gave us the authentic legend
of the caves: the boy, the girl, the forgotten lunch,
the mold. Ah, the mold! Excuse me, I have to put

my pain in the freezer. I'll shoulder the blame
for that. Sometimes it's enough to know
our old lovers are still out there. We'd prefer
not to see a recent picture or hear about

their cute children or their recent shoulder surgery
or their lifetime of success on the softball diamond

or the diamond futures trade. Only so many things
you can blame on pain pills. While I was at the freezer,

I got a lime popsicle. Lime popsicles are the best.
What do they put in them, lime or something?
Sometimes, it's that simple. My wife and I
stood on an overlook admiring the bridge—tall,

yes, very tall! But with a grace we could not
mock or ignore. The wind so strong
it swallowed our laughter. Blown backwards
with the others, we all struggled up

the scraggly path, as if we were not tourists,
just old friends trying to learn a new game.
We stood at the top while an old new friend
took our picture, clinging to each other

after 25 years of marriage. Behind us,
as beautiful and frightening as the imagination's
wedding dress, the bridge stood. I believe in
the gooey mess of soft cheese, the lifeline

of blue mold, the white sea. Mold is bad.
Mold is good. Free samples—we're digging in
while, behind glass, Rochefort wheels are rotated
by special Rochefort rotators who know at birth

just how far to turn them—it appears I've already
forgotten how to spell it. I'm blaming the drugs
again. It's hard to be patient. To be a patient.
To tell the truth so it matters. So that someone

doesn't actually shame you by calculating
your batting average. Thunder in the distance.
Thunder is the distance. We learn it once.
We learn it over and over. We are tested

on our knowledge, and we fail. Blame it
on lime popsicles. The smell after rain
might be the closest thing to heaven.
But how many other things have been

the closest things to heaven? Twenty-five
years ago, I forgot my sandwich in a cave.
Blown backwards, I'm having the time of my life
once again. Once again, and always.

The stitches will dissolve, or die trying.
How many times have you died trying?

ACKNOWLEDGMENTS

"Potato Skins," "Gun/Shy": *American Journal of Poetry*
"My Mother Advises Me to Get a Mani/Pedi": *AMP*
"Hale Bopp": *The Ampersand Review*
"The Secret Agent Briefcase": *Beyond*
"Spanning": *Big Muddy: A Journal of the Mississippi River Valley*
"Stuffing the Birds, Carnegie Natural History Museum": *Bloodroot*
"Strawberries and Mirrors": *Blue Lyra*
"Honorary Honor": *The Chariton Review*
"Final Miracle Before Retiring from Slowpitch": *The Cimarron Review*
"Declaring Bankruptcy," "Abandoned School in the Rain": *Crab Orchard Review*
"Miracles": *Diode*
"I Love Watching Rivers": *The Dunes Review*
"Legendary Toads": *Fail Better*
"Poison Control": *Fifth Wednesday*
"Hamburger Surprise": *Frontier Poetry*
"Still Life with Phone Booth," "Phone Booth, Eight Mile and Ryan": *Gargoyle*
"Unwritten Laws of Gravitational Isolation": *The Georgia Review*
"First Week Back After Stent": *Gingko Tree Review*
"Test Bomb Fallout": *Glass*
"Neighbor Down on Bridge": *Hubbub*
"Empty Nest," "My Father Worked 800 Hours of Overtime": *I-70 Review*
"On a Personal Level": *Labor*
"Shouting a Sonnet into Detroit's Dead Microphone": *Michigan Quarterly Review*
"Music of the Light Timer": *Natural Bridge*
"Property Value": *Nerve Cowboy*

"Leaving the Piano Behind": *Now Then* (Great Britain)

"High School Diploma, 1917," "Google Maps, Street View," "The Wound Doctor," "Searchlights Over Detroit": *The Paterson Literary Review*

"Between Double Doors": *Pembroke*

"Fishing in the Cement Pond": *Peninsula Poets*

"Fog on the Turnpike": *Pittsburgh Poetry Review*

"The New Math," "The Year of Burning," "Sunday Best": *Plume*

"Ripe Serviceberries": *Poetry Northwest*

"Midnight Football": *PoetryMagazine.com*

"The Grand Design": *Rattle*

"Annual Checkup with Money Specialist": *South Florida Poetry Journal*

"Bahia Honda, Key West": *The Tampa Review*

"Private Room": *32 Poems*

"My Daughter Turned Thirteen Today": *Tusculum Review*

"My Mother at the Sewing Machine," "Tying My Shoe at the New Pornographers Concert," "Wasting My Life, 3:00 a.m.,": *Two Bridges Review*

"Returning the Stones": *Wake: Great Lakes Thought and Culture*

"Harlem Globetrotters, Olympia Stadium": *Zocalo Public Square*